Nature Spotter
SEASHORE

CATHERINE BRERETON

Illustrated by
KATE McLELLAND

BLOOMSBURY
CHILDREN'S BOOKS
LONDON OXFORD NEW YORK NEW DELHI SYDNEY

BLOOMSBURY CHILDREN'S BOOKS
Bloomsbury Publishing Plc
50 Bedford Square, London, WC1B 3DP, UK
Bloomsbury Publishing Ireland Limited
29 Earlsfort Terrace, Dublin 2, D02 AY28, Ireland

BLOOMSBURY, BLOOMSBURY CHILDREN'S BOOKS and the Diana logo
are trademarks of Bloomsbury Publishing Plc

First published in Great Britain 2026 by Bloomsbury Publishing Plc

Text copyright © Bloomsbury, 2026
Illustrations copyright © Kate McLelland, 2026

All rights reserved. No part of this publication may be: i) reproduced or transmitted in any form, electronic or mechanical, including photocopying, recording or by means of any information storage or retrieval system without prior permission in writing from the publishers; or ii) used or reproduced in any way for the training, development or operation of artificial intelligence (AI) technologies, including generative AI technologies. The rights holders expressly reserve this publication from the text and data mining exception as per Article 4(3) of the Digital Single Market Directive (EU) 2019/790

A catalogue record for this book is available from the British Library

ISBN: 978-1-5266-9843-8

2 4 6 8 10 9 7 5 3 1

Text by Catherine Brereton

Printed and bound in China by Toppan Leefung Printing, DongGuan, GuangDong

To find out more about our authors and books visit
www.bloomsbury.com and sign up for our newsletters

For product safety related questions contact productsafety@bloomsbury.com

Published under licence from RSPB Sales Limited to raise awareness of the RSPB
(charity registration in England and Wales no. 207076 and Scotland no. SC037654).

For all licensed products sold by Bloomsbury Publishing Limited,
Bloomsbury Publishing Limited will donate a minimum of 2% from all sales to RSPB Sales Ltd,
which gives all its distributable profits through Gift Aid to the RSPB.

The RSPB is the UK's largest nature conservation charity. With your help,
they can protect wild spaces and create a bright future for wildlife.

FSC
www.fsc.org
MIX
Paper | Supporting
responsible forestry
FSC® C104723

CONTENTS

LET'S SPOT AT THE SEASHORE	4
HABITATS	5
CRUSTACEANS	6
JELLYFISH AND ANEMONES	10
MOLLUSCS	12
MAMMALS	16
WORMS AND REPTILES	20
BIRDS	22
SEA URCHINS AND STARFISH	28
INSECTS	32
FISH	36
SPONGES AND CORALS	42
SEAWEEDS	44
OUTDOOR ACTIVITIES	46

LET'S SPOT AT THE SEASHORE!

This book will help you spot and name many of the creatures you see by the seashore. There is so much to discover!

How to use your spotting guide
Each picture shows what the creature, seaweed or plant looks like – its shape, colour and patterns. Use the pictures to help you identify the wildlife you spot. Place the stickers on the matching pages each time you make a discovery!

The fact boxes display handy information. Here is the key:

🏠 tells you where the creature lives or where the seaweed or plant grows (habitat)

✏️ tells you the size of the animal, or the length of a fully-grown plant or seaweed

📅 tells you when you might see the wildlife. If you don't see a calendar, you can spot the wildlife all year round

Seashore-watcher rules
When you are watching wildlife, try to be quiet and still.
Don't drop litter, or pull up any seaweed.
Stay away from soft mud and dangerous cliffs.
Make sure you are always with an adult, and that they are aware of what time the tide is coming in and going out.

HABITATS

There are lots of places to look for exciting seashore wildlife!

Seashore and rock pools
The tide comes in and out twice a day revealing lots of wildlife. Rock pools provide shelter for some creatures.

Sand dunes
Sand dunes are made by the wind blowing sand from the sea. They are good habitats for flowers and insects.

Coastal grassland
Found along cliffs or inland from sand dunes, grasses are a great habitat for flowers and bees.

Estuaries
Estuaries are flat, muddy areas where a river meets the sea.

Salt marshes
These salty, muddy habitats are often flooded with saltwater.

Rocky cliffs
Cliffs are habitats for many seabirds, where they can shelter and nest. Cliffs are dangerous places for people to go – so take care!

Out at sea
The sea itself is full of life, from seabirds flying above to fish and corals living underwater.

Let's get spotting and sticking!

CRUSTACEANS

Crustaceans are a group of invertebrates that usually have a hard outside skeleton made up of armour plates or shells. Most have bodies made up of multiple sections.

60 cm

shallow seawater

Common lobster
The common lobster is a large, blue-black crustacean with 10 legs. Its front claws make fearsome weapons!

Lobsters use hairs on their front legs to taste food!

common lobster   sand hopper   common prawn

Sand hopper

2 cm

🏠
seashores, under stones

This tiny, pale creature lives under stones and in seaweed high up on the beach. It jumps in the air if it has been disturbed!

Look out for sand hoppers jumping on stones in the early evening.

Common prawn

The common prawn is found in rock pools but is hard to spot! It is see-through and can swim very fast.

11 cm

rocky seashores, rock pools

CRUSTACEANS

9 cm

rock pools, estuaries, shallow seawater

Shore crab
The shore crab has a front pair of powerful claws, which it uses to fight and catch its prey. It hides under stones in rock pools and comes out to hunt.

Hermit crab
The hermit crab doesn't have a shell of its own, so it finds an empty shell left behind by another creature and uses that!

3.5 cm

rock pools, rocky shores, shallow seawater

shore crab · hermit crab · common spider crab · edible crab

Common spider crab

20 cm

seashores, open sea

The common spider crab is a large orange or red crab with long legs. Every year, they migrate to deeper seas, and sometimes swim more than 160 km!

Edible crab

The edible crab is a large crab with black pincers. The edge of its shell looks like a pie crust.

25 cm

rocky shores, open water

JELLYFISH AND ANEMONES

Jellyfish have no brain, heart or blood.
Their bodies are 95 per cent water.

up to 40 cm

open sea

Moon jellyfish
The moon jellyfish has a see-through body that looks like an umbrella. Look out for it floating below the surface of the sea or stranded in a rock pool.

Jellyfish use their venomous tentacles to sting and catch their prey.

moon jellyfish   compass jellyfish   beadlet anenome

Compass jellyfish
The compass jellyfish has long, trailing arms and lots of fine tentacles. Beware – its tentacles can give you a nasty sting!

30 cm across

open sea

5 cm across

rock pools

Beadlet anenome
The beadlet anenome is a red, soft-bodied animal. It has a mass of stinging tentacles, which it uses to catch small creatures.

MOLLUSCS

Molluscs belong to a huge group of creatures called invertebrates, which are animals without a backbone. Molluscs have soft bodies and many of them have shells.

Common octopus

The common octopus is a large sea animal with eight strong arms. This expert predator wraps its prey in its arms and kills with a poisonous bite!

up to 130 cm

open sea, rocky and shallow coastal waters

Octopuses are some of the most intelligent invertebrates in the world.

common octopus   common squid   mussel

Common squid

This squid is pale white with a reddish-brown pattern. It has eight long arms and two even longer tentacles. It lives very deep underwater.

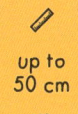

up to 50 cm

open sea

Mussel

The common mussel has a blue-black shell and a soft orange or beige body. It attaches itself to rocks with thin, strong threads known as a 'beard'.

3 – 10 cm

rocky, sandy or muddy shores and shallow seas

MOLLUSCS

6 cm

rocky shores

Common limpet
The common limpet has a cone-shaped shell. It clings onto rocks with a strong foot.

Its tongue is covered in tiny sharp teeth!

Flat periwinkle
These tiny sea snails find shelter in cracks in the rocks, amongst seaweed. They can have dark blue, black or brightly coloured shells.

up to 1.5 cm

seaweed on rocky and sandy shores

Common oyster

up to 11 cm

shallow coastal waters, estuaries

The common oyster has a grey or brown shell. The inside of the shell is pearly white. It is a filter feeder, mopping up scraps of dead animals and plankton in the water.

Common cockle

up to 5 cm

sandy shores, estuaries

The common cockle has a yellowish, white or brown shell. It has two feeding tubes. It sucks up water with one tube, and filters out food from the water. Then it uses its second tube to squirt out the leftover water.

MAMMALS

Mammals are warm-blooded animals. The mothers feed milk to their babies. Lots of mammals can live on the land and in the water. Other mammals, like whales and dolphins, spend their whole life in water.

Minke whale

up to 9 m

out at sea

The minke whale has a white band on its front flippers, a pointed head and grooves on its throat. It is considered small for a whale, despite being almost as long as a bus!

Its call sounds like a jet engine taking off.

Common seal

The common seal can be grey or sandy with dark spots. It basks on sandbanks or rocks with its head and tail up in the air.

up to 1.85 m

coastal rocks and beaches

over 2 m

rocks and beaches, out at sea

Grey seal

The grey seal is larger than the common seal. It is a browny-grey colour with a wide, flat head and a long snout. Its body shape is streamlined for swimming and hunting fish.

MAMMALS

up to 1.8 m

coasts, harbours, sometimes rivers

Common porpoise
The common porpoise, or the harbour porpoise, is about as long as an adult human. Like a dolphin, it breathes through a blowhole on top of its head.

Bottlenose dolphin
These pale grey dolphins swim in teams, rounding up fish. You may see them jumping out of the water or swimming alongside a boat.

up to 4 m

out at sea

common porpoise · bottlenose dolphin · orca

up to 9.8 m

out at sea

Orca

The orca is a giant predator and is a brilliant hunter. It is very intelligent and can communicate using squeaks, clicks and whistles.

Although the orca is sometimes called a 'killer whale', it is actually a dolphin.

WORMS AND REPTILES

Worms have thin, long, soft bodies without arms or legs. Reptiles breathe air and have scales or bony plates. Many reptiles lay eggs.

Lugworm

Lugworms live on sandy and muddy seashores. They swallow sand and filter out bits of food from it, then poo out the leftover sand.

up to 20 cm

muddy estuaries, sandy beaches

Look out for lugworm casts, like piles of sand spaghetti!

Tube worm

The tube worm builds itself a hard, white or grey tube on rocks or seaweed. The tiny worms hide away inside the casts.

up to 4 cm

rocky shores

 lugworm
 tube worm
 common lizard
 sand lizard

Common lizard

Common lizards are mostly brown with spots and stripes, but they can also be yellow, green and black. They stay very still and then run fast to catch insects to eat.

15 cm

sand dunes, cliffs, grasslands, woodlands, heathlands, moorlands

March – October

Sand lizard

Males are greenish with brown sides and females are brown all over. Both have two light stripes and dark spots on their backs.

20 cm

sand dunes, heathlands

April – October

BIRDS

Seas and rivers provide a rich source of food and shelter for many birds. The seashore can often be a great place to spot lots of noisy birds!

up to 60 cm

seaside, towns and cities, rivers, farmlands, wetlands

Herring gull
The herring gull has a grey back and wings, pink legs and a yellow beak with a red spot. They are protective parents and are skilled in finding food in lots of different habitats.

The herring gull has a loud, wailing cry.

herring gull   black-headed gull   great black-backed gull

Black-headed gull
This smallish gull is very noisy and likes to gather in a flock. The dark feathers on its head only appear in the breeding season.

37 cm

seaside, rivers, towns and cities, farmlands, wetlands

Great black-backed gull
The great black-backed gull might look like a herring gull, but it is bigger and has a black back instead of grey. It has a powerful beak.

78 cm

seaside, rivers, towns and cities, farmlands, wetlands

BIRDS

45 cm

coasts, estuaries, lakes, rivers

Oystercatcher
The oystercatcher is a big black-and-white bird with a bright orange beak. It pokes its beak into the sand to find shellfish to eat.

The oystercatcher uses its strong beak to open up mussels and cockles to eat.

 oystercatcher  curlew  avocet

Curlew

60 cm

coasts, estuaries, moorlands, farmlands

The curlew has a long, downward-curving beak. It uses its long beak to poke for crabs in mud or water. It is the largest wader around the UK coastline.

Avocet

The avocet is a black-and-white wader. It has long legs, like stilts. Look out for it sweeping its long bill to snap up small creatures in estuaries and lagoons.

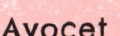
45 cm

coasts, wetlands, grasslands

BIRDS

Puffin
The puffin is a black-and-white seabird with a colourful beak. On land it waddles about, but it can fly very fast and swim strongly underwater.

 29 cm

 sea cliffs, open sea

 April – July

A puffin can hold over 100 sandeels in its mouth at once!

 39 cm

 sea cliffs, open sea

 March – July

Razorbill
The razorbill is a medium-sized seabird. It can dive hundreds of metres below the surface to catch fish!

puffin | razorbill | cormorant | common tern

Cormorant

 100 cm

 sea, lakes, rivers

The cormorant is a large bird and an expert fisher. Look out for one sitting on a rock with its wings stretched out.

Common tern

The common tern dives to catch fish for its young. It will 'dive bomb' any animal that tries to attack the colony – even a fox!

 35 cm

 wetlands, inland, seaside

 April – September

SEA URCHINS AND STARFISH

Sea urchins are spiny creatures that live on the ocean floor. They use their spines to move across the seabed. Starfish usually have five pointed arms and are found in shallow waters and deep sea.

5 cm

coastal seawater, deep sea

Green sea urchin
The green sea urchin is a ball-shaped, spiny animal. It is usually green and purple. Its stiff spines protect it from predators.

If you are paddling in the sea, take care not to step on an urchin — you may get spikes in your feet!

Edible sea urchin

up to 15 cm

🏠
rock pools, rocky shores

The edible or common sea urchin is often pink or purple, but can be red, green or yellow. Look out for it in rocky parts of the seashore.

skeleton

You might find an urchin skeleton on the beach!

Sea potato

sea potato shell

The sea potato is a sea urchin that is the shape and colour of a potato! It has fine, brown spines that look like hairs.

up to 9 cm

sandy and muddy seabeds, seashores

SEA URCHINS AND STARFISH

Common starfish

The common starfish is red or orange, and has five arms in a star shape. It hunts shellfish and uses its strong arms to pull their shells open.

up to 30 cm across

sandy beaches, rock pools, open sea

Starfish have two stomachs!

up tp 70 cm

open water

Spiny starfish

The spiny starfish is a pale grey-green colour and has five very long arms covered in big spines. It is the UK's largest starfish.

Common sunstar

up to 35 cm

seabed in shallow waters and deep water

This starfish looks like the sun! It is a predator and likes to eat worms, sea cucumbers, sea urchins and even other sunstars!

Common brittlestar

The common brittlestar is a small starfish with five very long bristly arms. Its arms can break off easily if it is disturbed or threatened, but they will always grow back!

2 cm across (legs 10 cm long)

rock pools, open sea

INSECTS

Insects are a type of small animal that have six legs. Lots of them have wings. They are the largest group of animals on Earth.

Southern hawker
The southern hawker is a fast flier. You might see it on shores around lakes or pools of water.

7cm

ponds, lakes, canals, woodlands

June – October

up to 3 cm

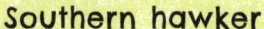
grasslands, freshwater, wetlands, woodlands

May – September

Common blue damselfly
The common blue damselfly has a thin, dainty body. Males are bright blue and females can be bright blue or dull green.

southern hawker • common blue damselfly • long-winged conehead • green tiger beetle

Long-winged conehead

Look for this bright green cricket hopping, or listen for it buzzing, in grassy sand dunes. It has a cone-shaped head and long wings and legs.

2 cm

grasslands, wetlands, farmlands, freshwater

May – October

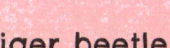

Green tiger beetle

This shiny green beetle is a fierce hunter with powerful jaws and a fast sprint. It runs along chasing spiders, ants and caterpillars to eat.

1.5 cm

sand dunes, grasslands, woodlands

April – September

INSECTS

Common blue

The common blue is a small butterfly. The male has lilac-blue wings. The female is brown, but some have blue markings. They like warm, sunny, grassy places including sand dunes.

3.5 cm wingspan

gardens, meadows, woods, sand dunes

May – October

Grayling

The grayling is a dark brown butterfly with orange patches. Look out for it gliding around in sand dunes and near cliffs.

6 cm wingspan

sand dunes, heathlands, saltmarshes, cliffs

June – September

common blue · grayling · red-banded sand wasp · cliff mining bee

Red-banded sand wasp

This large, thin wasp lives alone at the seashore and on heathland. Female sand wasps sting caterpillars and then lay their eggs inside the caterpillars' bodies.

2.5 cm

sandy shores, heathlands

June – September

Cliff mining bee

The cliff mining bee has a furry reddish thorax and a smooth black abdomen. Females dig nest tunnels in seaside cliffs, quarries and riverbanks.

1.5 cm

cliffs, sandy grasslands

March – August

FISH

Fish are animals that live in water. They breathe through gills and have fins instead of legs.

Basking shark

The basking shark is a huge, dark grey shark with a giant mouth. It keeps its mouth wide open as it swims along.

up to 12 m

open sea, shallow bays

May – October

A basking shark can weigh up to seven tonnes. That's more than three cars!

basking shark   sand goby   common blenny

Sand goby

10 cm

shallow sea, estuaries, saltmarshes

This small, pale brown fish is found in sandy pools. It has a slender body and a thin head.

Common blenny

The common blenny hides in rock pools. Look out for its thick lips which help it crush hard shells.

up to 17 cm

rock pools in summer, open sea in winter

It uses the little fins underneath its body to climb as well as swim!

FISH

Common goby

6 cm

rock pools, estuaries, sea

The common goby is a small fish found in rock pools. It has sandy colouring, so is well camouflaged against sand and pebbles.

Many fish in rock pools have suckers to hold onto rocks when the tide rushes in and out.

Tompot blenny

The tompot blenny has an orangey body, big eyes and frilly-looking tentacles on its head that look like antlers.

up to 30 cm

shallow seas, rock pools

The male fish guards the eggs until they hatch safely.

Common goby   tompot blenny   rock goby   butterfish

Rock goby

The rock goby is brown with black blotches. It likes to eat small prawns, crabs and worms.

12 cm

shallow seas, rocky waters

25 cm
rock pools

Butterfish

The butterfish is a long-bodied eel-like fish that hides under stones and seaweed in rock pools. It gets its name because it is slimy and slippery to hold, like butter!

FISH

Shore clingfish

This orangey-red spotty fish has a mouth that looks like a duck's beak. It clings onto rocks with a strong sucker-like fin.

7 cm

shallow waters, rock pools

April – October

Worm pipefish

The worm pipefish is long and very thin. It looks like a long brown strand of seaweed, so it can hide well.

up to 15 cm

rocky shores, seaweed

April – October

shore clingfish · worm pipefish · shore rockling · sea stickleback

Shore rockling

The shore rockling is found in rock pools. It has three bristles around its mouth to feel for prey such as worms and tiny crustaceans.

25 cm

rocky shores, rock pools

April – October

Sea stickleback

25 cm

shallow waters, rock pools, estuaries

This long, thin fish is found in rock pools and shallow seawater. It has 14 – 17 spines on its back and is also known as the 15-spined stickleback.

SPONGES AND CORALS

A sea sponge is an animal without a brain, lungs or heart. They hardly move at all. A coral is not a single animal but a colony of tiny animals living as one. Together they build hard or soft skeletons.

Sea orange sponge

10–40 cm

seawater, attached to rocks or sea wreckage

The sea orange sponge looks rubbery with holes. It sucks up water through the holes and filters particles of food from the water.

Breadcrumb sponge

The breadcrumb sponge looks a bit like a crumbly crust of bread! It grows on rocks and seaweed stalks.

up to 100 cm

rocky shores, rock pools,

sea orange sponge · breadcrumb sponge · dead man's fingers · pink sea fan

up to 25 cm tall

rocky surfaces under the sea

Dead man's fingers
This soft coral looks like it has fingers! It can be orange, brown, white or pink, and sticks out stinging tentacles to catch animals.

Corals are under threat from pollution, human activity and temperature rises.

Pink sea fan
The pink sea fan is pink, orange or white and shaped like a frilly fan. It is a hard coral, which means it has a rocky skeleton.

up to 50 cm

shallow waters

SEAWEEDS

Seaweed is the name for the brown, green and dark red marine algae that lives in the sea or on coastal rocks. Unlike land plants, seaweed doesn't have roots.

Sugar kelp

up to 5 m

rocky shores

This brown seaweed looks like a wide belt with ruffled edges. It likes sheltered places and is found in deep pools and on the lowest parts of the shore.

It gets its name from the sweet white powder that is released when the seaweed dries.

 sugar kelp  sea lettuce  gutweed

Sea lettuce

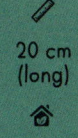

20 cm (long)

seashores, rock pools

This bright green seaweed looks like a big bunch of lettuce! It is so thin that it is see-through, and like many other seaweeds, it is edible.

Gutweed

Gutweed looks like soggy, green grass. It gets its name because when bubbles of air get trapped in the strands, it blows up and looks like intestines in the human gut!

up to 40 cm

rock pools, seashores

45

OUTDOOR ACTIVITIES

Try these activities when you are spotting on the seashore!
Reward yourself with a sticker each time you try a new activity.

Go rock pooling
You will need:
- a bucket
- a magnifying glass
- a notebook and pencil

Instructions:
1. Find a rock pool on the seashore.
2. Lift up a few pebbles to see if there is anything underneath.
3. Carefully use your bucket to scoop out water. Don't have too many creatures in the bucket at once – they might eat each other!
4. Use your magnifying glass to get a closer look.
5. Draw or write about what you have seen.
6. Always put the creatures back into the rock pool, and replace any seaweed or pebbles you have moved.

Keep safe!
Rock pools can be slippery, and the water may be deep.
Some animals can nip and sting.
Ask an adult before touching anything with your hands.

Sand and shell art

Go shell hunting and play around with sand to create some amazing beach art!

- Collect shells of all shapes, sizes and colours and make fun patterns in the sand. You could make a shell heart, a big shell spiral or spell out a secret message!
- Grab a stick and draw a picture or write your name in the sand. You could decorate with shells and pebbles.
- Use fine, wet sand to mould together and make sculptures. You could make a starfish or even a shark!

Take a photo of your design before the tide washes it away.

A big beach clean

Our seashores are under threat from plastic pollution. Can you help with a big clean to clear up rubbish on the beach?

Follow the rules!
- Always have a grown-up with you on any beach clean.
- Wear protective gloves and don't pick up or touch anything sharp.

The safest way to help is to join an organised beach clean. Find out more here:
www.mcsuk.org/what-you-can-do/join-a-beach-clean

NATURE SCRAPBOOK

Your seashore spotting adventures don't have to stop here. Why don't you create your own nature record book? All you need is a notebook, some pencils and an outdoor adventure!

How to make your book

- Draw pictures or take photographs of the interesting animals, seaweed and shells you spot.
- Create a written record for each spot, including: name of wildlife, date and time, where you found them and any fun facts.
- Use your 'Just for fun' stickers to decorate your book.

Bloomsbury Publishing Plc does not have control over, or responsibility for, any third-party websites referred to in this book. All internet addresses in this book were correct at the time of going to press. The author and publisher regret any inconvenience caused if addresses have changed, but can accept no responsibility for any such changes.